Spotlight on the Philippines

Bobbie Kalman

🌳 Crabtree Publishing Company

www.crabtreebooks.com

Spotlight On My Country

Created by Bobbie Kalman

For Charles Eiffert in the Philippines,
and his father Heinz,
who is lost somewhere on this planet

**Author and
Editor-in-Chief**
Bobbie Kalman

Editors
Kathy Middleton
Crystal Sikkens

Fact editor
Marcella Haanstra

Design
Bobbie Kalman
Katherine Berti
Samantha Crabtree (cover)

Photo research
Bobbie Kalman

**Print and production coordinator
and prepress technician**
Katherine Berti

Illustrations
Bonna Rouse: page 9

Photographs
Big Stock Photo: pages 11 (top left),
 15 (top)
Wikipedia: Joshua Lim: page 13
 (middle right)
Other images by Shutterstock

Library and Archives Canada Cataloguing in Publication

Kalman, Bobbie, 1947-
 Spotlight on the Philippines / Bobbie Kalman.

(Spotlight on my country)
Includes index.
Issued also in electronic format.
ISBN 978-0-7787-3463-5 (bound).--ISBN 978-0-7787-3489-5 (pbk.)

 1. Philippines--Juvenile literature. I. Title. II. Series: Spotlight
on my country

DS655.K34 2011   j959.9   C2011-900005-9

Library of Congress Cataloging-in-Publication Data

Kalman, Bobbie.
 Spotlight on the Philippines / Bobbie Kalman.
   p. cm. -- (Spotlight on my country)
 Includes index.
 ISBN 978-0-7787-3489-5 (pbk. : alk. paper) -- ISBN 978-0-7787-3463-5
(reinforced library binding : alk. paper) -- ISBN 978-1-4271-9686-6
(electronic (pdf))
 1. Philippines--Juvenile literature. I. Title. II. Series.

DS655.K35 2011
959.9--dc22

2010051452

Crabtree Publishing Company

www.crabtreebooks.com   1-800-387-7650

Printed in the U.S.A./022011/CJ20101228

**Published in Canada
Crabtree Publishing**
616 Welland Ave.
St. Catharines, Ontario
L2M 5V6

**Published in the United States
Crabtree Publishing**
PMB 59051
350 Fifth Avenue, 59th Floor
New York, New York 10118

**Published in the United Kingdom
Crabtree Publishing**
Maritime House
Basin Road North, Hove
BN41 1WR

**Published in Australia
Crabtree Publishing**
386 Mt. Alexander Rd.
Ascot Vale (Melbourne)
VIC 3032

Contents

A country in Asia

The Philippines is a **country** made up of more than 7,000 **islands**. A country is an area of land with **borders**. An island is land that has water all around it. The Philippines is located in the southeast part of the **continent** of Asia. A continent is a huge area of land. The other continents are North America, South America, Europe, Africa, Australia/Oceania, and Antarctica. The seven continents are shown on the map below. The Philippines is near the **equator**. The equator is an imaginary line around the middle of Earth where the sun's rays are the strongest. Areas near the equator have a **tropical** climate, which means it is warm year round.

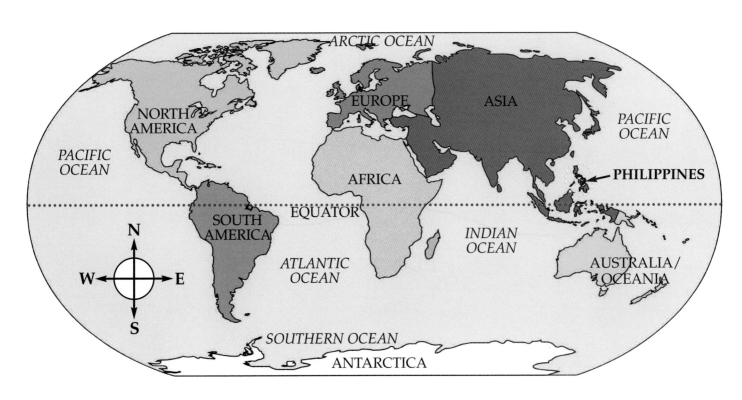

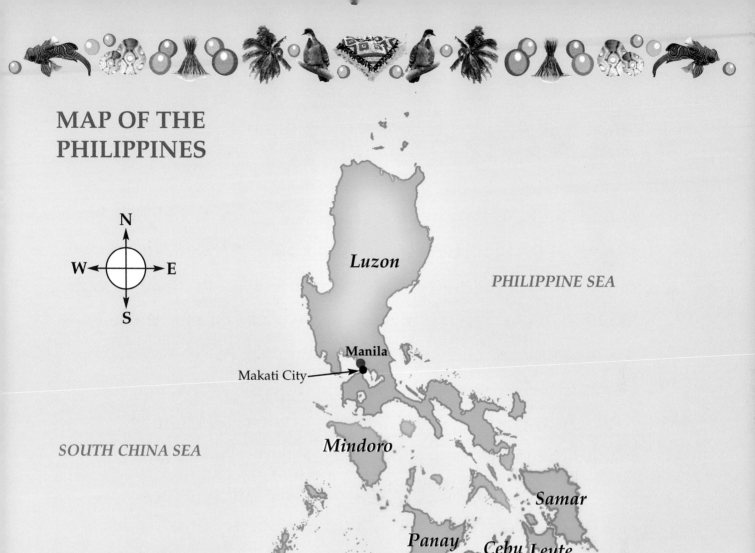

MAP OF THE PHILIPPINES

N
W — **E**
S

Luzon

PHILIPPINE SEA

Manila

Makati City →

SOUTH CHINA SEA

Mindoro

Samar

Panay

Cebu **Leyte**

Cebu City●

Palawan

Negros **Bohol**

SULU SEA

Mindanao

Davao City●

MALAYSIA

CELEBES SEA

5

Islands and seas

The thousands of islands of the Philippines form an **archipelago**. An archipelago is a chain of islands in a body of water, such as an ocean. The Philippines Archipelago is in the western Pacific Ocean in Southeast Asia. It is surrounded by clear blue **seas** and **straits**. A sea is part of an ocean near land. A strait is a narrow passage of water between two big bodies of water or areas of land.

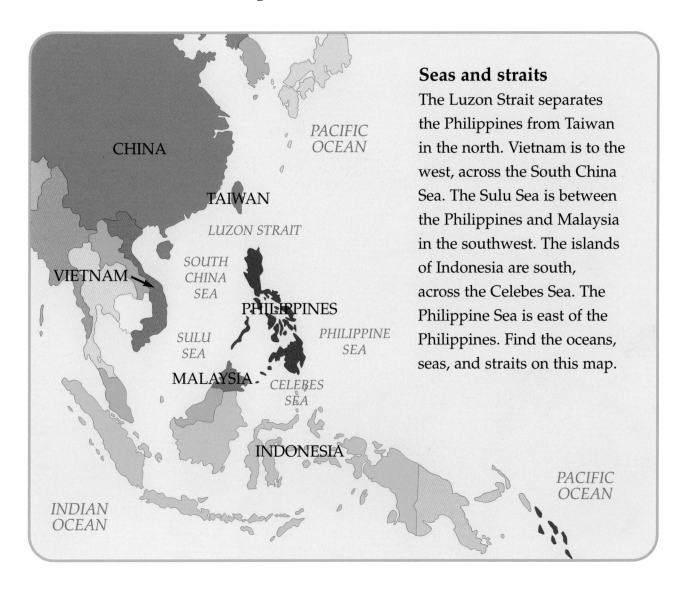

CHINA

PACIFIC OCEAN

TAIWAN

LUZON STRAIT

SOUTH CHINA SEA

VIETNAM

PHILIPPINES

PHILIPPINE SEA

SULU SEA

MALAYSIA

CELEBES SEA

INDONESIA

PACIFIC OCEAN

INDIAN OCEAN

Seas and straits

The Luzon Strait separates the Philippines from Taiwan in the north. Vietnam is to the west, across the South China Sea. The Sulu Sea is between the Philippines and Malaysia in the southwest. The islands of Indonesia are south, across the Celebes Sea. The Philippine Sea is east of the Philippines. Find the oceans, seas, and straits on this map.

The main island groups

The Philippines has three main island groups: Luzon, Mindanao, and Visayas. Luzon, in the north, is an island group as well as the biggest island. Mindanao, in the south, is an island group and the second-largest island. The Visayas is an **archipelago**, or chain of islands. The island groups are further divided into regions, provinces, and cities.

*Palawan Island is part of the Luzon island group, Mimaropa region, and Province of Palawan. It is the biggest of more than 1,700 islands that belong to Palawan Province. Palawan Island has beautiful beaches, clear water, and fantastic **rock formations**. Rock formations are rocks with unusual shapes.*

Philippine facts

The Republic of the Philippines has a **population** of about 95 million people. Over eight million Filipinos live in other countries around the world. The people speak two main languages—Filipino and English. The capital city of the country is Manila. The president is the leader of the country.

*People gathered in Manila at the **inauguration**, or introduction, of President Benigno Aquino III, on June 30, 2010. He is the 15th president of the country.*

What is a republic?

The government of the Philippines is a **republic**. In a republic, the citizens of the country **elect**, or choose, their leader. The people of the Philippines vote for a new president every six years. The president is the head of the government.

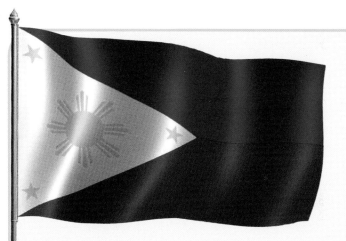

The flag

The flag of the Philippines has a blue band, a red band, and a white triangle. Blue stands for truth and justice. Red is for bravery. The white triangle stands for equality and brotherhood. The triangle has a sun with eight rays representing the first provinces, as well as three stars representing the three island groups. When the Philippines is at war, the flag is turned upside down, and the red band is at the top.

The people of the Philippines are called Filipinos.

Who are the Filipinos?

Tagalog woman

The Philippines is home to people of many backgrounds. Most are **descendants** of the Malay, who came to the Philippines thousands of years ago from Malaysia and Indonesia. The Tagalog make up one-quarter of the country's population and live mostly in Manila, where they work in factories, banks, and other businesses. The second-largest group is the Cebuano. Most Cebuano live on the island of Cebu, but some live on the other islands, as well.

Many Cebuano live in large cities, whereas others dwell in the countryside, where they farm or fish for a living. This young Cebuano man and his dog are enjoying a day at the beach.

This man is part of the Higaonon Tribe. The Higaonon are native people who live in the northern parts of the island of Mindanao. Their name means "people of the living mountains."

About one in every ten Filipinos has Chinese **ancestry**. Ancestry means being related to a line of people who came before you.

The Ifugao people live on mountainsides, where they grow rice. These Ifuago people are riding home on a crowded bus called a **jeepney**.

Maranao peoples live mostly on Mindanao. The Maranao are Muslims. Muslims follow the religion of Islam. This Maranao woman is performing a dance at a festival.

11

The main cities

There are 122 cities in the Philippines. Most of these are part of **metropolitan** areas. A metropolitan area is a city and the areas around it. The largest city in the Philippines is its capital city, Manila. Metropolitan Manila is made up of sixteen cities. Its area has a population of more than twenty million people. Other big cities are Cebu City and Davao City. Davao City is the largest city on the island of Mindanao.

The City of Makati is one of the 16 cities that make up Metropolitan Manila. Makati is the business center of the Philippines and one of the business centers of Asia. It has a population of more than a half million people.

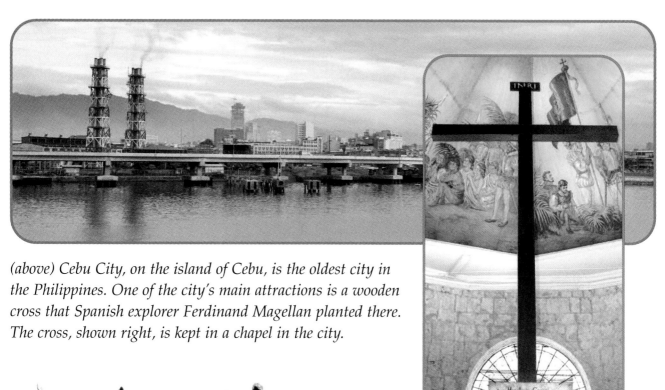

(above) Cebu City, on the island of Cebu, is the oldest city in the Philippines. One of the city's main attractions is a wooden cross that Spanish explorer Ferdinand Magellan planted there. The cross, shown right, is kept in a chapel in the city.

This peace monument is in Davao City in Mindanao. An angel and dove, a priest, a lumad (a native person) and a moro (Muslim) stand for the three ethnic and religious parts of Mindanao.

13

Farming and fishing

Many Filipinos work in the cities, but many others live in the countryside and work as farmers and fishers. Farmers grow a variety of vegetables and fruits, but rice is the main part of the Filipino diet. It is grown in **paddies**, or special rice fields. Farmers grow the **seedlings**, or young rice plants, in fields near the paddies.

*Rice is grown on flooded land. This farmer stands in water all day planting rice seedlings. The Ifugao people grow rice on the sides of mountains. The Banaue Rice Terraces, shown below, have been named a **World Heritage Site**.*

This Filipino farmer and his family are returning from a day of working in the fields. The children also help with the farm work. The family lives on the island of Mindanao.

Fishing is a big source of food in the Philippines. Fishers in small boats catch fish to feed their families. Fishers on big boats catch fish to sell. Tuna, anchovy, sardine, grouper, and snapper are some of the fish they catch. At night, fishers use lanterns to attract fish to the water's surface. These fishers are in Filipino boats called bankas.

The Ring of Fire

The Philippines is in the "Ring of Fire" area. More than half of Earth's active **volcanoes** are in the Pacific Ocean in this area. A volcano is an opening in Earth's **crust**, or outer layer, which allows hot magma, ash, and gases to escape from below the earth. The Philippines has 50 volcanoes, 18 of which are **active**. Active volcanoes are volcanoes that can erupt at any time. Most of the Philippines islands were formed from volcanoes. Mount Pinatubo, Mount Mayon, and the Taal Volcano are active volcanoes. They are all on Luzon.

*Mount Mayon is the most active of the Philippines volcanoes. In 1814, lava from the Mayon volcano spilled over the village of Cagsawa, destroying the whole village. Only the top of the church remains. When Mayon erupted again in 2009, 33,000 people had to be **evacuated**, or removed from the area.*

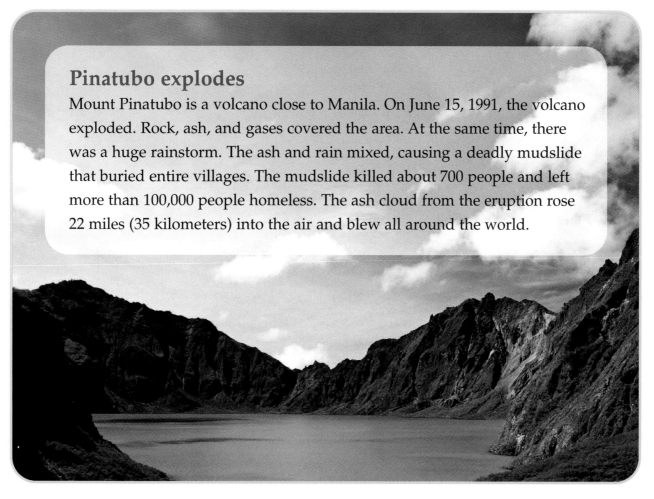

Pinatubo explodes

Mount Pinatubo is a volcano close to Manila. On June 15, 1991, the volcano exploded. Rock, ash, and gases covered the area. At the same time, there was a huge rainstorm. The ash and rain mixed, causing a deadly mudslide that buried entire villages. The mudslide killed about 700 people and left more than 100,000 people homeless. The ash cloud from the eruption rose 22 miles (35 kilometers) into the air and blew all around the world.

*When Mount Pinatubo exploded, its top collapsed and formed a **caldera**, or huge pit. The pit filled with water and created a lake. The lake is called Lake Pinatubo. Read more about calderas below.*

After a large eruption, a volcano cannot hold up the mountain above it. Cracks form around the edges, and the center of the volcano falls inward, forming a caldera. Over time, a caldera fills with rainwater and turns into a lake. The Taal volcano is an island located in a caldera that is actually inside another caldera. This caldera was formed by a very large eruption long ago.

17

Water everywhere!

Beginning in May, strong winds called **monsoons** carry the moisture from oceans over the country. These winds bring the wet season, which lasts until November. Heavy rains fall during the wet season, and the air becomes **humid**, or damp. March, April, and May are the hottest months. From June to November, Filipinos watch for dangerous **typhoons**. Typhoons are violent, whirling windstorms that are like hurricanes. As many as 25 or more typhoons can strike the Philippines in one year. Typhoons destroy homes, ruin crops, and cause terrible floods.

Typhoon Ondoy brought flooding to this village on the island of Luzon in 2009, causing hundreds of thousands of people in the area to lose their homes. In 2010, an even stronger typhoon, Megi, struck the Philippines. This super typhoon hit the northern part of Luzon.

Earthquakes and monster waves

Many earthquakes are caused by volcanic activity, and there is plenty of activity in the Ring of Fire! When earthquakes happen under water, they can cause giant waves called **tsunamis**. Tsunamis smash into the coasts of the islands. They can carry away anything in their path and flood the land the way typhoons do. The Philippines can be as dangerous as it is beautiful!

People's lives are turned upside down after a typhoon, tsunami, or earthquake. These natural disasters make life difficult for people living in the Philippines, especially if they have lost their homes, possessions, and friends or family members.

Nature's beauty

The Philippines is beautiful—both on land and in the water. The amazing sights of this country include rain forests, mountains, **lagoons**, waterfalls, and amazing rock formations. These pages show some of these land and sea wonders.

lagoon

These rock formations and this lagoon are on Palawan. A lagoon is an area of calm water separated from an ocean by islands or **coral reefs** *(see pages 22–23).*

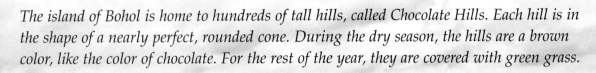

The island of Bohol is home to hundreds of tall hills, called Chocolate Hills. Each hill is in the shape of a nearly perfect, rounded cone. During the dry season, the hills are a brown color, like the color of chocolate. For the rest of the year, they are covered with green grass.

waterfalls

The Philippines is close to the equator, so the weather is warm year round. Rain forests with tall trees grow on the land.

Most of the Philippine islands have high mountains. Rice is often planted on the sides of the mountains. Waterfalls crash down the mountainsides.

Coral reefs

Close to the islands of the Philippines are beautiful coral reefs. Coral reefs are ocean habitats with many kinds of fish and other animals. The animals you see on these pages can be found in the coral reefs of the seas around the Philippines. Some amazing and weird sea animals live in these ocean habitats.

*Coral reefs are found near the shores of warm oceans. They are made up of corals. Corals look like colorful plants, but they are not plants. They are groups of tiny animals called **coral polyps**. Many coral reefs are found near islands. This reef is very close to shore, where the water is shallow. The reef's plants and animals get plenty of sun.*

mandarinfish

Mantis shrimp are not shrimp. They belong to the same animal family as crabs and lobsters. Mantis shrimp are **predators**, or animals that hunt and eat other animals. They eat shrimp and other small ocean animals. A mantis shrimp mother carries her eggs in a pouch under her body, as shown above.

boxfish

Many **species**, or types, of sharks glide by the coral reefs in the Philippines. The whale shark is one of them. This shark is the world's largest fish. It is so big that it looks like a whale! Whale sharks swim with their giant mouths open, so they can catch many fish to eat at once. This shark has its mouth full!

Mandarinfish and boxfish are two colorful fish that swim in the coral reefs of the Philippines.

Animals on land

Many kinds of amazing animals live on land, as well. The Philippine tarsier is an **endangered** species of tarsier found only on the southern islands of the Philippines. An endangered animal is in danger of dying out. The tarsier is just six inches (15 cm) long and is one of the smallest **primates**. It lives high in trees and comes out only at night to hunt. Its large eyes help it see in the dark, and its neck turns almost all the way around to look for predators or for insects to eat. A tarsier has a long tail that helps it balance when climbing and leaping through the trees. The tips of its fingers are like suction cups. Having sticky fingers makes it easier to hold on while climbing.

Philippine eagles are more than 36 inches (about 1 meter) tall. They hunt monkeys, flying squirrels, and large snakes.

The Mindanao bleeding heart is a kind of pigeon that lives only in the Philippines. Why do you think it is called by that name?

The binturong is also known as a bearcat, but it is not a bear or a cat. This animal lives in the rain forests of many Asian islands, including the Philippines. It is active at night and sleeps on branches during the day. It eats mainly fruit, but it also eats eggs, mice, and birds.

Religions of the country

Religion is a very important part of life in the Philippines. Most Filipinos take part in religious ceremonies and celebrate holy days with big festivals. The majority of Filipinos practice the Christian religion. The second-largest number of people follow the religion of Islam. A few Filipinos are Buddhists, some follow Taoist beliefs, and still others are **animists** who pray to the spirits in nature.

Christianity is a religion based on the teachings of Jesus Christ, whom Christians believe is the son of God. About 81 percent of Filipinos belong to the Roman Catholic Church. The large number of Christians in the Philippines makes this country one of the biggest Christian countries in the world. It is also one of only two Asian countries where Christianity is the main religion. Churches can be found almost everywhere in the Philippines—even on beaches!

There are many religious festivals and parades. This young boy is carrying a cross in the Roman Catholic Black Nazarene parade in Manila.

Muslims follow the religion of Islam. Their place of worship is called a mosque. Most Filipino Muslims live on Mindanao.

The Taoist Temple in Cebu City was built by Cebu's large Chinese community. Taoism is a belief practiced in China. The followers of Taoism pray at the Taoist Temple, but people of all faiths are welcome. Twice a week, people climb the 81 steps of the temple to worship there.

Filipino cultures

Today, many different groups of Filipino peoples make their home on the islands. Each group speaks its own language and practices its own customs, traditions, and religions. The **culture** of the Philippines combines the customs, arts, music, beliefs, and languages of the different groups. People from other countries have had a strong influence on Filipino culture, as well. Spain ruled the Philippines for over 300 years. It brought the Christian religion to the country. The United States then ruled the country for 48 years and brought the English language to the Philippines.

This parade float shows a time when the Spanish ruled the Philippines. The float includes a Catholic church.

English	Filipino
Welcome! or Long life!	*Mabuhay!*
Good morning	*Magandang umaga*
Good afternoon	*Magandang hapon*
Good evening	*Magandang gabi*
How are you?	*Kumusta ka?*
I'm fine.	*Mabuti naman.*
Please	*Paki or Bigyan ng kasiyahan*
Thank you	*Salamat*
You're welcome.	*Walang anuman.*
Yes	*Oo*
No	*Hindi*
Okay	*Sige*
I don't know.	*Hindi ko alam.*
What is your name?	*Anong pangalan mo?*
My name is _____.	*Ako si _____.*

Kumusta ka?

In Filipino, there are two ways to speak to someone—a polite, formal way and a casual way. Practice these "friendly" Filipino phrases with your friends. What is the boy saying?

This Filipino boy is singing an American song. Americans brought their language and culture to the Philippines. The Chocolate Hills are behind the boy. Could he be singing a sweet song about candy or chocolates?

Celebrating culture

Parades are a part of many Filipino **fiestas**, or festivals. The Aliwan Fiesta celebrates the different regions and cultures of the Philippines. It takes place in Pasay City, one of the cities in metropolitan Manila. The Fiesta started in 2003 and is held in April or May. There are three parts to the fiesta: a cultural dance competition, a float parade, and a beauty pageant. The costumes are works of art!

Each of the country's 17 regions sends people to represent them in dance, parade, and beauty.

The costumes are very colorful and beautiful!

Will this exciting parade float win a prize?

This drummer plays music at the fiesta.

Will this beautiful girl be a pageant winner?

31

Glossary

Note: Some boldfaced words are defined where they appear in the book.

active Describing a volcano that has erupted recently or may soon erupt

border An imaginary line that separates countries or areas of land

coral polyp A tiny ocean animal with a soft round body and tentacles around its mouth

coral reef An area of an ocean that is made up of live coral polyps and dead corals

endangered Describing an animal or plant species that is in danger of dying out

equator An imaginary line around the center of Earth

lagoon Shallow ocean water that is separated from the open ocean by land or a coral reef

predator An animal that hunts another animal for food

primates A group of mammals with large brains, including humans, chimpanzees, and monkeys

rock formation A rock with an unusual shape

species A group of closely related living things that can make babies together

strait A narrow area of water that connects two large areas of water

tropical Describing areas with hot climates found near the equator

tsunami A giant wave created by an earthquake or volcanic eruption underwater

typhoon A violent tropical storm

volcano An opening in Earth's crust where hot lava, gases, ash, and rocks shoot out

World Heritage Site A natural or cultural place that is important to human beings

Index